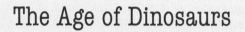

The Age of Dinosaurs

Meet Ornitholestes

Written by Jayne Raymond
Illustrations by Leonello Calvetti and Luca Massini

Cavendish
Square

New York

Published in 2014 by Cavendish Square Publishing, LLC
303 Park Avenue South, Suite 1247, New York, NY 10010

Website: cavendishsq.com

This publication represents the opinions and views of the author based on his or her personal experience, knowledge, and research. The information in this book serves as a general guide only. The author and publisher have used their best efforts in preparing this book and disclaim liability rising directly or indirectly from the use and application of this book.

CPSIA Compliance Information: Batch #WW14CSQ

All websites were available and accurate when this book was sent to press.

Library of Congress Cataloging-in-Publication Data

Raymond, Jayne.
Meet ornitholestes / by Jayne Raymond.
p. cm. — (The age of dinosaurs)
Includes index.
ISBN 978-1-62712-613-7 (hardcover) ISBN 978-1-62712-614-4 (paperback) ISBN 978-1-62712-615-1 (ebook)
1. Ornitholestes — Juvenile literature. I. Raymond, Jayne. II. Title.
QE862.S3 D35 2014
567.913—dc23

Editorial Director: Dean Miller
Art Director: Jeffrey Talbot
Designer: Joseph Macri
Photo Researcher: Julie Alissi, J8 Media
Production Manager: Jennifer Ryder-Talbot
Production Editor: Andrew Coddington

Illustrations by Leonello Calvetti and Luca Massini.

The photographs in this book are used by permission and through the courtesy of: Gallo Images/the Agency Collection/Getty Images, 8; Ryan Somma/Ornitholestes hermanni - American Natural History Museum/Flickr/Creative Commons Attribution-Share Alike 2.0 Generic License, 20; Design Pics/Peter Langer/Peter Langer/Newcom, 21.

Printed in the United States of America

CONTENTS

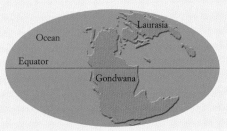
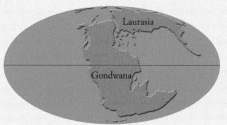
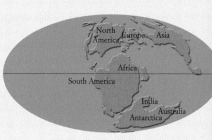

| Late Triassic | Early Jurassic | Middle Jurassic |
| 227 – 206 million years ago. | 206 – 176 million years ago. | 176 – 159 million years ago. |

A CHANGING WORLD

Earth's long history began 4.6 billion years ago. Dinosaurs were among the most fascinating animals from the earth's long past.

The word "dinosaur" originates from the Greek words *deinos* and *sauros* and which together mean "fearfully great lizards."

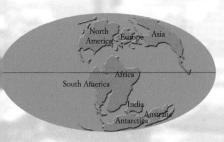
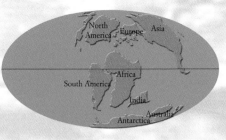

Late Jurassic	Early Cretaceous	Late Cretaceous
159 – 144 million years ago.	144 – 99 million years ago.	99 – 65 million years ago.

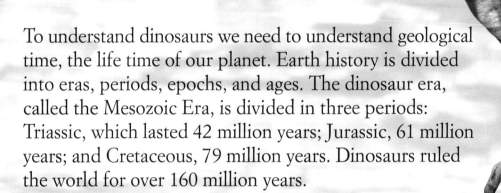

To understand dinosaurs we need to understand geological time, the life time of our planet. Earth history is divided into eras, periods, epochs, and ages. The dinosaur era, called the Mesozoic Era, is divided in three periods: Triassic, which lasted 42 million years; Jurassic, 61 million years; and Cretaceous, 79 million years. Dinosaurs ruled the world for over 160 million years.

Man never met dinosaurs. They had disappeared nearly 65 million years before man's appearance on Earth.

The dinosaur world differed from our world. The climate was warmer, the continents were different, and grass did not even exist!

A SMALL PREDATOR

Ornitholestes belongs to the order Saurischia (or lizard-hipped) and the suborder Theropoda that lived on Earth between the Late Triassic and the end of the Cretaceous period, from 228 to 65.5 million years ago.

The name
Ornitholestes comes
from the Greek and means
"bird robber" which refers to the fact
that, according to the paleontologist who
named it, such a frail predator could only eat
small animals, such as birds, which it could
catch with its long forelimbs.

Ornitholestes was no more than six feet (1.8 m) long and about a foot and a half (0.5 m) high at the hip. It was one of the smaller dinosaurs, and it has been estimated that it weighed 20–25 pounds and had a very long tail. Only one species is known: Ornitholestes hermanni.

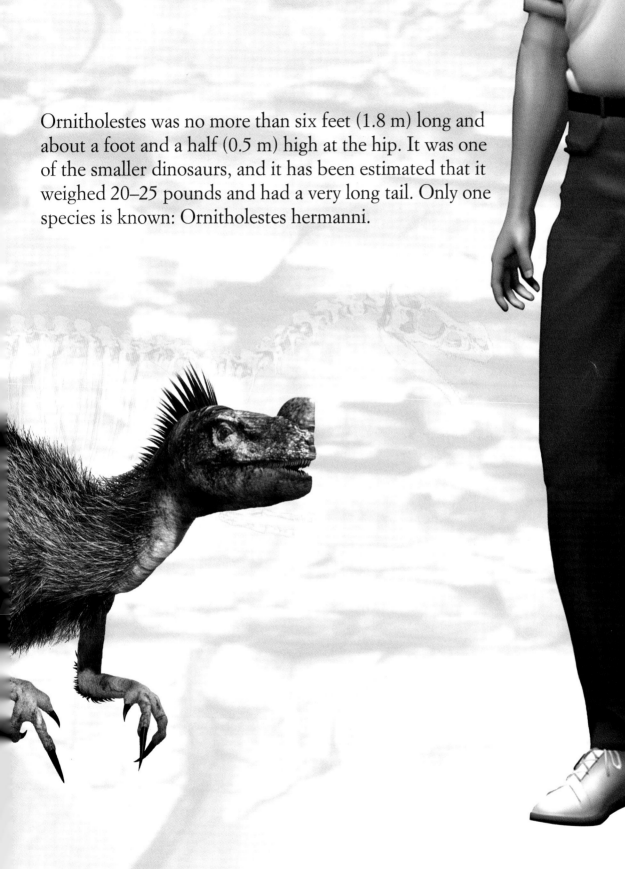

FINDING ORNITHOLESTES

It lived in North America at the end of the Late Jurassic period, 155–148 million years ago, hunting in plains similar to the present African savanna, where the giant plant-eating sauropods such as Diplodocus and Camarasaurus and the great predators such as Allosaurus and Ceratosaurus lived at the same time. Its remains have so far been discovered only in the Jurassic sandstone of Wyoming.

Wyoming, U.S.A.

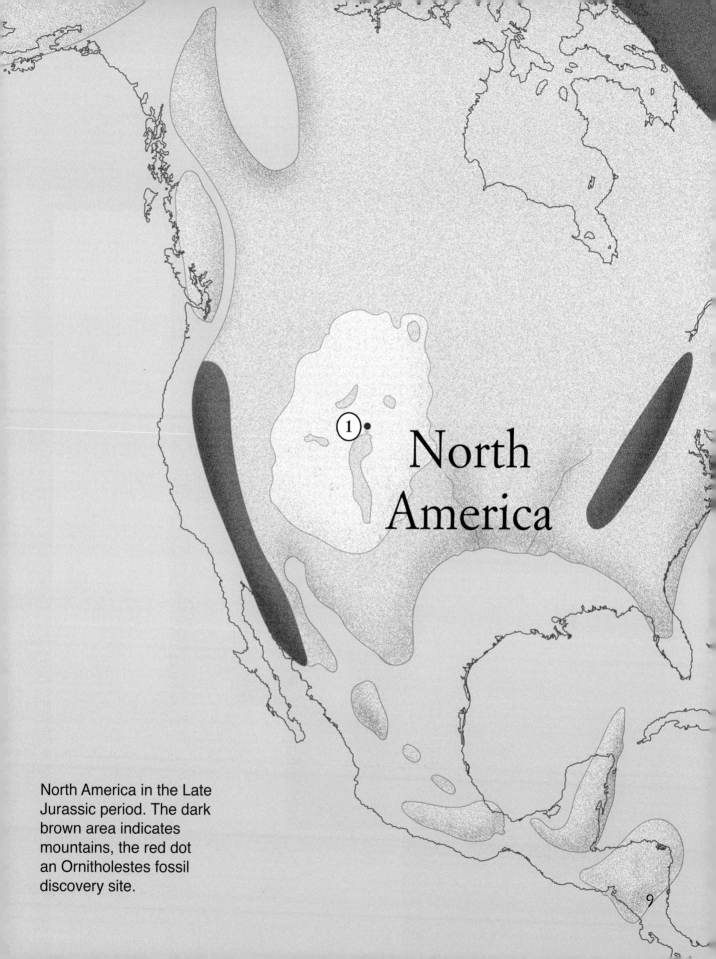

North America

North America in the Late Jurassic period. The dark brown area indicates mountains, the red dot an Ornitholestes fossil discovery site.

BIRTH

We can only guess what the Ornitholestes eggs and nests looked like, because no fossil remains have been found. They may have been like other small theropods that lived later, such as Troodon, Velociraptor, and Oviraptor. Ornitholestes may already have known how to build an open nest, round and with a raised mud rim, like that of Troodon and some of the present-day birds.

STEPPING OUT

The only prey the baby Ornitholestes could hope to catch must have been insects or small reptiles. The American savanna of 150 million years ago was overrun with small animals the dinosaur could catch: lizards, sphenodonts (lizard-like reptiles), primitive frogs, salamanders, and tiny mammals similar to shrews and rats. They may also have eaten fish that they caught in brooks and rivers.

RUSH HOUR

The vast plains where Ornitholestes lived were populated
by large animals such as the sauropods. These immense
dinosaurs, often more than 65 feet (19.8 m) long, wouldn't
even have noticed the small biped theropod, which was
a danger only to their eggs and hatchlings. Ornitholestes
instead had to watch out so the huge plant-eating dinosaurs
wouldn't squash them under their big feet.

15

FEEDING TIME

Even though it was decidedly small, Ornitholestes was still a predator. An adult might well hunt a helpless small plant-eating dinosaur such as Othnelia. Also, the young of the larger dinosaurs might fall victim to Ornitholestes if their parents were not on guard.

17

INSIDE ORNITHOLESTES

The fossil skeleton of the only specimen of Ornitholestes found to date consists of a skull with the lower jaw and the teeth, numerous vertebrae of the neck, trunk, sacrum, and tail, the entire pelvic girdle, and part of the fore and back limbs. Even though it is incomplete, it is an articulated skeleton.

The skull was about half a foot long and probably had a small crest or horn at the end of the snout. The front teeth were conical while the others were serrated like a knife for cutting meat. The row of teeth on the lower jaw was shorter than that on the upper jaw.

The thighbone was not even a foot long. Some paleontologists have suggested that Ornitholestes may have been swift runners.

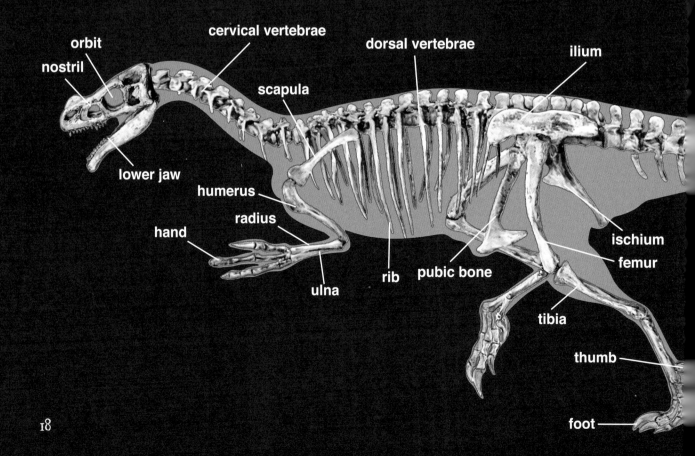

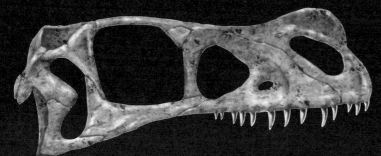

Side view of the skull

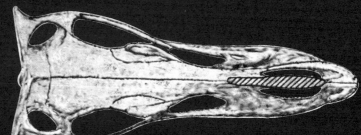

Dorsal view of the skull

caudal
vertebrae

chevron

FINDING ORNITHOLESTES FOSSILS

The only specimen of Ornitholestes was found in Bone Cabin Quarry in Wyoming during an excavation campaign by the American Museum of Natural History in 1900. It is mounted and on exhibit in the museum in New York City.

The Bone Cabin Quarry site is known for the great quantity of bones of gigantic dinosaurs—above all sauropods—found there, a fossil hunter's dream.

The Ornitholestes specimen was studied and named by the paleontologist Henry Fairfield Osborn in 1903. Initially Osborn had reconstructed it with a neck and body that were longer than it should have been, but he later corrected his first reconstruction.

Discovery sites of
the Coelurosaurians
figured below

● Coelurus, United
States, 155–148
million years ago

◆ Compsognathus,
Germany and France,
150 million years ago

COELUROSAURIANS

Small relatively primitive theropods such as Ornitholestes have been found in Jurassic and Lower Cretaceous rocks, although they are rather rare. Recently it was discovered that Coelurus and Ornitholestes are closely related.

Scipionyx, Italy, 110 million years ago

Ornitholestes, United States, 155-148 million years ago

THE GREAT EXTINCTION

Sixty-five million years ago (about 80 million years after the time of Ornitholestes), dinosaurs became extinct. Scientists think a large meteorite hitting the earth caused this extinction. A wide crater caused by a meteorite exactly 65 million years ago has been located along the coast of Mexico. The dust suspended in the air by the impact would have obscured the sunlight for a long time, causing a drastic drop in temperature and killing many plants.

The plant-eating dinosaurs would have starved or frozen to death. Meat-eating dinosaurs would have also died without their food supply. However, some scientists believe dinosaurs did not die out completely, and that present-day chickens and other birds are, in a way, the descendants of the large dinosaurs.

A DINOSAUR'S FAMILY TREE

The oldest dinosaur fossils are 220–225 million years old and have been found all over the world.

Dinosaurs are divided into two groups. Saurischians are similar to reptiles, with the pubic bone directed forward, while the Ornithischians are like birds, with the pubic bone directed backward.

Saurischians are subdivided in two main groups: Sauropodomorphs, to which quadrupeds and vegetarians belong; and Theropods, which include bipeds and predators.

Ornithischians are subdivided into three large groups: Thyreophorans which include the quadrupeds Stegosaurians and Ankylosaurians; Ornithopods; and Marginocephalians sub-divided into the bipedal Pachycephalosaurians and the mainly quadrupedal Ceratopsians.

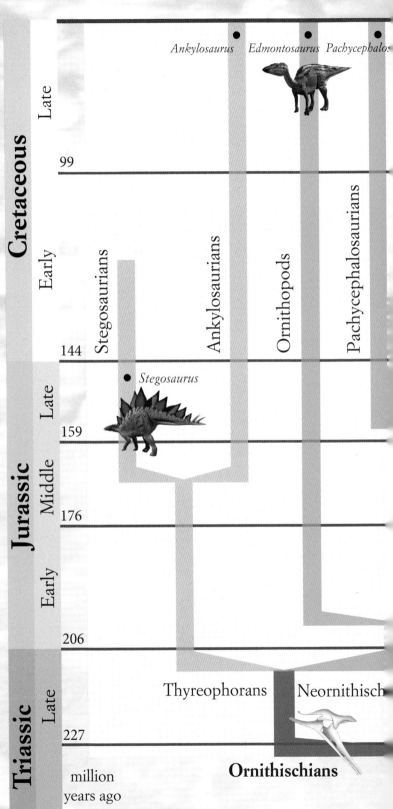

Ankylosaurus *Edmontosaurus* *Pachycephalos*

Stegosaurians

Ankylosaurians

Ornithopods

Pachycephalosaurians

• *Stegosaurus*

Thyreophorans   Neornithisch

Ornithischians

Cretaceous	Late	
		99
	Early	
		144
Jurassic	Late	
		159
	Middle	176
	Early	
		206
Triassic	Late	
		227

million years ago

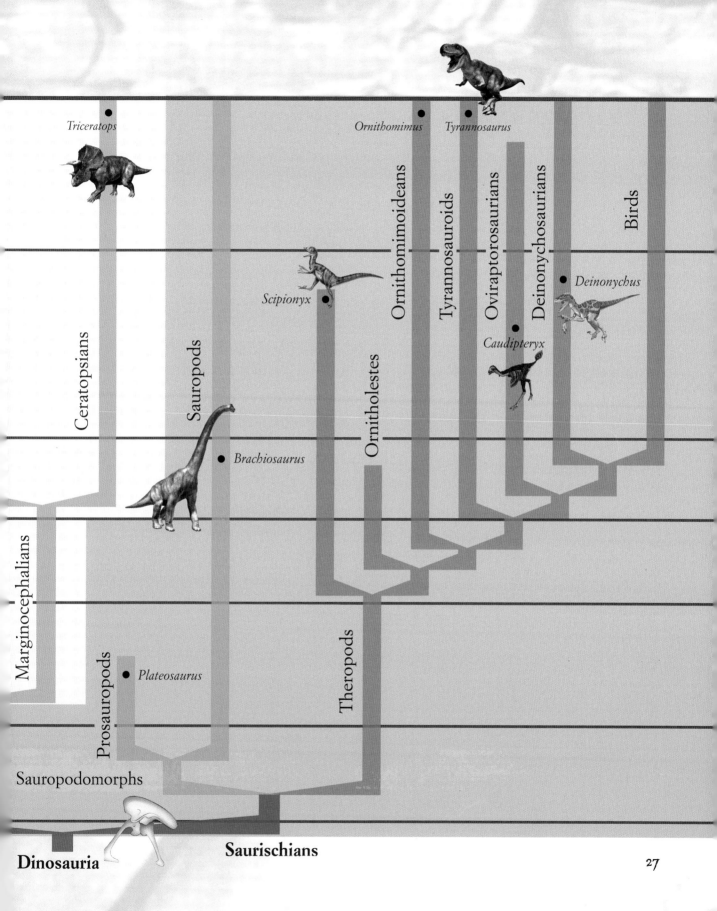

Triceratops

Ornithomimus   Tyrannosaurus

Ornithomimoideans

Tyrannosauroids

Oviraptorosaurians

Deinonychosaurians

Birds

Ceratopsians

Sauropods

Scipionyx

Deinonychus

Ornitholestes

Caudipteryx

Brachiosaurus

Marginocephalians

Theropods

Prosauropods

Plateosaurus

Sauropodomorphs

Dinosauria

Saurischians

A SHORT VOCABULARY OF DINOSAURS

Bipedal: pertaining to an animal moving on two feet alone, almost always those of the hind legs.

Bone: hard tissue made mainly of calcium phosphate; single element of the skeleton.

Carnivore: a meat-eating animal.

Caudal: pertaining to the tail.

Cenozoic Era (Caenozoic, Tertiary Era): the interval of geological time between 65 million years ago and present day.

Cervical: pertaining to the neck.

Claws: the fingers and toes of predator animals end with pointed and sharp nails, called claws. Those of plant-eaters end with blunt nails, called hooves.

Cretaceous Period: the interval of geological time between 144 and 65 million years ago.

Egg: a large cell enclosed in a porous shell produced by reptiles and birds to reproduce themselves.

Epoch: a memorable date or event.

Evolution: changes in the character states of organisms, species and higher ranks through time.

Feathers: outgrowth of the skin of birds and some other dinosaurs, used in flight and in providing insulation and protection of the body. They evolved from reptilian scales.

Forage: to wander in search of food.

Fossil: evidence of the life in the past. Not only bones, but footprints and trails made by animals, as well as dung, eggs or plant resin, when fossilized, is a fossil.

Herbivore: a plant-eating animal.

Jurassic Period: the interval of geological time between 206 and 144 million years ago.

Mesozoic Era (Mesozoic, Secondary Era): the interval of geological time between 248 and 65 million years ago.

Pack: a group of predator animals acting together to capture the prey.

Paleontologist: scientists who study and reconstruct the prehistoric life.

Paleozoic Era (Paleozoic, Primary Era): the interval of geological time between 570 and 248 million years ago.

Predator: an animal that preys on other animals for food.

Raptor (raptorial): a bird of prey, such as an eagle, hawk, falcon, or owl.

Rectrix (plural rectrices): any of the larger feathers in a bird's tail that are important in helping its flight direction.

Scavenger: an animal that eats dead animals.

Skeleton: a structure of animal body made of several different bones. One primary function is also to protect delicate organs such as the brain, lungs, and heart.

Skin: the external, thin layer of the animal body. Skin cannot fossilize, unless it is covered by scales, feathers, or fur.

Skull: bones that protect the brain and the face.

Teeth: tough structures in the jaws used to hold, cut, and sometimes process food.

Terrestrial: living on land.

Triassic Period: the interval of geological time between 248 and 206 million years ago.

Vertebrae: the single bones of the backbone; they protect the spinal cord.

DINOSAUR WEBSITES

Dinosaur Train (pbskids.com/dinosaurtrain/): From the PBS show Dinosaur Train, you can have fun watching videos, printing out pages to color, play games, and learn lots of facts about so many dinosaurs!

The Natural History Museum (http://www.nhm.ac.uk/kids-only/dinosaurs/): Take a quiz to see how much you know about dinosaurs or a quiz to tell you what type of dinosaur you'd be! There's also a fun directory of dinosaurs, including some cool 3D views of your favorites.

Discovery Channel Dinosaur videos (http://dsc.discovery.com/video-topics/other/dinosaur-videos): Watch almost 100 videos about the life of dinosaurs!

Dinosaurs for Kids (www.kidsdinos.com): There's basic information about most dinosaur types, and you can play dinosaur games, vote for your favorite dinosaur, and learn about the study of dinosaurs, paleontology.

DinoData (www.dinodata.org): Get the latest news on dinosaur research and discoveries. This site is pretty advanced, so you may need a teacher's or parent's help to find what you're looking for.

MUSEUMS

Yale Peabody Museum of Natural History, 170 Whitney Avenue,
New Haven, CT 06520-8118

American Museum Natural History, Central Park West at 79th
Street, New York, NY 10024-5192

The Field Museum, 1400 South Lake Shore Drive, Chicago, IL
60605-2496

Carnegie Museum of Natural History, 4400 Forbes Avenue,
Pittsburgh, PA 15213-4080

National Museum of Natural History, the Smithsonian Institution,
10th Street and Constitution Avenue NW, Washington, DC
20560-0136

Museum of the Rockies, 600 W. Kagy Boulevard, Bozeman,
MT 59717

Denver Museum of Nature and Science, 2001 Colorado Boulevard,
Denver, CO 80205

Dinosaur National Monument, Highway 40, Dinosaur, CO 81610

Sam Noble Museum of Natural History, 2401 Chautauqua,
Norman, OK 73072-7029

Museum of Paleontology, University of California, 1101 Valley Life
Sciences Bldg., Berkeley, CA 94720-4780

Royal Tyrrell Museum of Palaeontology, Highway 838, Drumheller,
AB T0J 0Y0, Canada

INDEX

Page numbers in **boldface** are illustrations.

....